THE RECIPE

HEARING GOD'S Voice

SAINT SHENOUDA PRESS

THE RECIPE

HEARING GOD'S Voice

Peter Fahim

Foreword by:
Fr Meena Awad

ST SHENOUDA PRESS
SYDNEY, AUSTRALIA
2025

The Recipe
By: Peter Fahim

Copyright © 2025
St. Shenouda Press

All rights reserved. Except for brief quotations in critical publications or reviews, no part of this book may be reproduced in any manner without prior written permission from the publisher.

St Shenouda Press
8419 Putty Rd,
Putty, NSW, 2330
Sydney, Australia

www.stshenoudapress.com

ISBN 13: 978-1-7638415-6-7

All scripture quotations, unless otherwise indicated, are taken from the New King James Version®. Copyright © 1982 by Thomas Nelson, Inc. Used by permission. All rights reserved.

Special Thanks

Special thanks to the team at **Parable Podcast** for pouring so much heart and hard work into bringing this book to life. Your care, creativity, and persistence shaped this project in ways that go far beyond production.

Contents

Foreword 1

It Starts Here.. 3

Chapter One: The Background Story 5

Chapter Two: The Crazy Story I Asked For..........14

Chapter Three: The Recipe 24

Chapter Four: The Map..31

Chapter Five: The Tools 38

Chapter Six: A Heart that is Eternal 48

Foreword

When you think of reading, you imagine sitting somewhere quiet with a coffee, a blanket, maybe a candle and disappearing into the page. What you probably don't imagine is reading a book that makes you want to lace up your shoes and start doing push-ups.

But that's exactly what this book does.

Somehow, Peter has managed to pack so much energy into these pages that you don't feel like a passive reader… you feel like a participant. This isn't a book you simply consume, it's a book that provokes, invites, and trains. It's spiritual exercise.

And yes, there is a recipe, just not one that teaches you how to make the perfect omelette or bake sourdough. This is a recipe for the other kind of strength: the kind that grows real spiritual muscle. The kind that doesn't just toughen your body but awakens your heart to hear God with clarity and walk with Him in confidence.

I love how practical, tangible, and beautifully simple it is. No theological riddles. No spiritual gymnastics. Just an honest, real-world guide that speaks straight into a universal struggle many of us face at some point in our lives.

Because for so many, hearing God feels mysterious,

reserved for the elite "spiritual people." But here, Peter breaks that lie. He shows how hearing God isn't complicated... It's achievable. It's meant for ordinary people like you and me.

Reading this feels less like instruction and more like someone taking your hand and saying, "Come on, I'll show you." And as you follow along, you find yourself becoming lighter, encouraged, sharpened, almost without realising it.

So yes, get comfortable. Grab your tea. Sit down...

But don't be surprised if halfway through you suddenly feel the urge to stand up, to stretch, to pray, to listen, to act. Because this book will move you.

It's time to train. Not physically though no one's stopping you from doing push-ups between chapters but spiritually.

It's time to build those inner muscles and step into the vibrant relationship with God that has always been yours.

Fr Meena Awad

It Starts Here...

Have you ever been in a hard situation and been told to ask God What He thinks?

Have you ever been stuck or had to make a difficult decision and the advice was to go and get God's opinion?

I've had those two lines said to me many times growing up and it used to drive me crazy because I had no idea how to hear His voice.

Is He supposed to speak in an audible voice?

Lost. That was my situation until I finally heard Him and I am writing this to share with you how I got there. Not because my story is overflowing with wisdom and mind-boggling experiences, but because we overcome him (the evil one) with the blood of the lamb and the power of our testimony. Also, God doesn't just use our testimony to overcome the evil one but to reach out to those who think they're alone and weak in their situation.

It Starts Here...

Here is a quick fact: you are not the only one and YES it helps to surround yourself with a body of believers who are willing to open up about their weaknesses.

He is so faithful to use our weaknesses to inspire strength.

It's crazy how Paul once said that he boasted in his weakness. What?! How? We have repeated that verse so many times it has become dull. Can you believe that, as Christians, we gain strength from our weakness? Not only that, He uses the weak to put to shame the strong. So with all the power and authority that Satan has, he is going to be put to shame with our weakness?! Yes! We have authority because it was given to us when we became God's children. So tell him off!

Keep reading and I'll explain how this works.

Chapter One

The Background Story

And so it all began...

September 7th, 2006 was my first day in the German University in Cairo. I was so excited to etch my path in engineering but it seems God had other plans. Rather than my university years being about growing in knowledge it was my faith that began to be tested.

I grew up in a Christian household, went to church every week and when I was old enough I was asked to minister to the Sunday school class. (You know how it works). I didn't smoke, drink or do drugs and never dated (I was waiting for the one). In case you aren't Egyptian and don't know, 12% of the Egyptian population are Christians which gave me bonus 'heaven-points' for being a good

Christian boy in a Muslim country.

After my first year I got a chance to go to Germany and study there which was the first time for me to live on my own. (I've traveled a lot throughout my life but never lived alone). Being busy with school, visiting different places in Europe and making new friends meant there was no time to be the good Christian boy I thought I was and spend time with God. (At least that's what I told myself.)

Time went by and I started to feel like I missed church, and thought, "Maybe I should start attending a church or even go back into ministry. After all, I need to bring people to Christ!"

Then it hit me. Why don't I take my friends and go to church! The next time I saw them I presented the idea of maybe going to church that Sunday and attending a service. Their response shocked me. My friend Mark said, "Peter, we don't believe in God!"

I erupted, "WHAT? You don't believe in God? How? The one who created THE heavens and THE earth! Who created you! Who created the crazy details that you can see around you! How can you not believe in Him?"

Let me explain something. Being Egyptian comes with a package. Every Egyptian has their religion on their ID This is for several reasons:

1. People inherent their religion (if you convert away from Islam you die).

2. It needs to be known if you are Christian or not, as Christians don't have same rights living in a Muslim country (like being in some government positions).

3. The system doesn't have the option of being an atheist.

Hence, growing up, I had never known an atheist or at least someone who could say it out loud...

At that moment I felt that I was given an assignment from heaven. I need to convert my friends. They have to know Jesus!

So I sat them down, brought out my Bible and told them that we needed to talk. I spent hours talking to them about who Jesus is and God's plan for the universe. I started with creation and went through the gospels. I went on and on about what Jesus has been doing and is doing. I talked about His love and mercy and how we can have a relationship with Him. Finally, I shared with them about how we need

Jesus and His salvation in order to have eternal life and not burn in hell ! The message was solid.

After I was done there were a few moments of silence.

Crickets

Then Mark laughed and said, "Peter, my friend, I have a question for you. Have you ever experienced any of what you've read in the Bible? Have you ever been healed or seen healing? Have you ever heard God speak?"

Then, I was quiet.

Crickets act 2

I was trying to answer his question honestly. So I asked myself, have I really experienced God? Have I ever even heard Him speak before?

I answered Mark saying, "Actually no, I don't think I've ever heard Him or seen any of what the Bible says about Him!"

So Mark asked me, "Then why are you wasting your time believing in someone who isn't real? Who needs God anyway, science can explain everything."

That night I left confused.

I wasn't sure why I had never felt or heard God before. It took me several days to figure out where I stood but, after much thought, I took my Bible and threw it in a street garbage can.

I had decided that there was no God.

And from that point on it was easy for me to move forward. Everything I wanted to do... I did. If I felt bad because it was wrong I told myself there was no need to feel that way because I no longer believed in God, therefore, there was no need to please Him.

However, this only seemed to confuse me further so I created some rules for myself based on values I felt would help me remain content with my way of living. I needed to be a good citizen and make sure people liked me.

I'm happy with that!

So, I went to a bar every night and tried every drink they had. I was making up for lost time! Since I had never dated, I started looking for a girlfriend to make me feel loved. Funnily enough, I was still scared to do anything beyond kiss a girl (I believe that God always had a plan). I went to clubs, tried singing and dancing all night while drinking and discovered I had a horrible voice and my dancing wasn't much better (of course, being tipsy made me carefree).

I kept this up until I had to go back to Cairo, which I wasn't happy about because I knew I could never enjoy my life in such a conservative country. I also had to deal with family and friends asking me why

I wasn't going to church or why I wasn't going back into ministry.

A few months passed and people had started to figure out that I had changed and were slowly giving up on me. One of my leaders tried to stay in touch with me, but I told him, "Bassem I appreciate you keeping in touch with me but if you feel this will somehow get me to see the love of Jesus through you then don't waste your time, man! I am over that Christian propaganda."

Bassem replied, "Peter all I want is to have lunch with you every now and then and see how you're doing."

To be honest I was ok with that. Who says no to

a free meal?

Not long after, Bassem's business was on the decline. He was losing a lot of money but had decided to believe that God would make a move in his life and save the day. That was total madness to me! He was waiting for someone who didn't exist to do something impossible.

Bassem cried out to the Lord everyday asking Him to intervene. However, Bassem's situation did not improve and he was falling deeper into debt.

One night, a friend of mine named Nader called me and said, "Peter aren't you friends with Bassem?" I replied, "yes."

Then Nader said, "I have a message for him. Tell him that while he was in the prayer meeting last night I saw, in the spirit, an angel giving him a check that is going to arrive on the 1st of December."

I exclaimed, "WHAT? Heck no! Why would I tell him a lie?"

I hung up with Nader, angry that people weren't helping Bassem in more practical ways. Why would they tell him fairy tales knowing that he could end up in jail? I called Bassem to check up on him and when he answered I could tell from his voice that

The Background Story

things were not ok. I found out that things had started going south more rapidly and all I could say to help was, "Bassem, by the way, Nader called me and said that last night, at the prayer meeting, he saw an angel giving you a check that will arrive December 1st."

There wasn't much conversation after that and the call ended. What did I just do? I felt guilty and decided not to call him again. I decided that when he did go to prison I would visit him and support him emotionally.

I am guessing you guys now have an idea how this story ended.

Well, HE decided to send Bassem the money on time and the fun part was that I witnessed the whole thing. HE wanted me to know that someone was up there looking out for His kids. That He was a practical God. Now I know what some of you may say…

Nader could have told someone to give the money to Bassem on that date. True! BUT the crazy part wasn't the timing or the money anymore…it was the amount.

Bassem didn't know exactly how much he

needed. He may have known the debt he owed but not the amount needed for the paperwork or the fines in total. The money that was given was exact down to the pound.

Chapter Two

The Crazy Story I Asked For

That was pretty much the end of the story for Bassem but it made me wonder. What if Nader wasn't high on drugs when he called me?

Is God actually that involved in our lives?

I had to think again. What if there is a God?

I mean logically speaking…. I would rather believe in God and be wrong than not believe and end up in hell. Might as well give it one more shot and find out if He is actually there.

The story made me reassess what I believed in. But I knew I needed more. I wanted another story but this time more personal.

The Recipe

During that same week, I was in my room sitting in bed and praying "God if You are real, alive and want a personal relationship with me, I ask that You would show yourself to me! I don't care which religion You belong to. Just allow me to know You. Amen."

I opened my eyes, but now what? Was He going to speak to me? Was He going to appear to me? I needed to know what to do next. Should I just wait?

A few days passed and I was getting impatient. I decided to put myself in an environment where I knew He would be present. So, I began attending a revival meeting where people didn't know me (which is hard because in Cairo everyone knows everyone). It was only bit-by-bit that the words in the sermons started to touch me. Sometimes it would just sound good but at other times it would move my feelings. Only this time I was skeptical. I didn't want to go back to believing something because it's what I was told growing up.

So I questioned everything.

Of course some of my questions didn't have answers but neither did science.

Still, in my heart, I was waiting for my own crazy story. That this God up there would reach out to me. After all, this was the last chance I was giving Him. I just wanted to be fair I guess.

Now, to be honest, the meeting was a little bit too much for me! There were always people praying in tongues, falling and afterwards chatting about their visions and dreams. Because I'd never been a part of something like this it offended me and when I went and asked the pastor about the gifts, he said I should just focus on Jesus and not worry about them. After a while, I reached a point where I was ready to leave the meeting altogether. Those people were crazy!

It was during that same period of time that my car broke down. I took it to the mechanic and discovered it needed a part replaced so I went with a friend to a street in Egypt known for mechanical parts. We went around on foot and asked every shop for the part I wanted, and nothing! It was as if they stopped making gas filters for Fiats! Some of the responses included, "I haven't seen it in a while" or "we ran out". There were a few shops left on the street and I was starting to stress out. I found myself unintentionally saying, "Please God, help me find it!"

Here's the crazy part... I said that while I was

The Recipe

standing on the island in the middle of the road and for some reason I froze. I think there were two things happening in that moment; one - I was surprised I was calling out to Him for help without being fully on board yet and two - I actually couldn't move (later on I found out this was called a trance). It was like I was watching a movie.

I saw myself crossing the road, heading to a shop and asking the shopkeeper, "Do you have a gas filter for my Fiat?"

He responds, "I don't think so."

Then I find myself saying, "Can you please look inside your storage? I really need it."

He looks at me with a bothered face and says, "Ok friend."

As he gets up to go to the storage, he knocks a glass off the table and says, "Don't worry about it, it's old." He goes in the back and a few seconds later returns with the filter and says it'll be 35 pounds (about 7 dollars).

I then came to myself, still standing on that island, and my friend was screaming back at me from the other side saying, "Dude what's wrong with you? Did you forget how to cross the street?"

The Crazy Story I Asked For

(If you haven't been to Egypt before, crossing streets in Cairo is a touch more dangerous than anywhere else. Google it.)

When I crossed over to the pavement I still wasn't sure what had just happened but I recognized the shop two shops down. So I pulled my friend and went inside. We found the shopkeeper sitting at a table. He asked us, "How can I help you?"

I responded, "I'm looking for a gas filter for my Fiat." He shook his head and said, "I don't think I have it."

Suddenly I started to see what was going on. Is this the part where I ask him if he's ok looking in the storage in the back? I was quiet and my friend had already started moving away towards the next shop. I don't know why but I was afraid, maybe because deep down I knew this was the crazy story I had asked for.

So I asked the shopkeeper, forcing the words out of my mouth, "Can you please see if you have any in your storage?"

As he got up he hit a glass and it shattered on the floor. I had goose bumps running up my neck to the point where I was shivering.

The Recipe

He said, "Don't worry about it, it's old anyway."

I guess you know what happened next. I paid him the 35 pounds because he had found the part I needed.

I needed a moment so I called David, a friend of mine whom I had met at this meeting I was going to, and I told him what had just happened. I told him

I wasn't sure what was going on but that I felt God had just given me my personal crazy story.

At this point I knew that He had kept His end of the bargain- He gave me that personal story I had asked for. I knew that my next step was to know Him more. Maybe He would reach out again and, if I became a Christian again, maybe this time it would be real.

So I went home and decided to start reading the Bible. I actually remember making this decision many times before and only ever getting through Genesis every month because I would start, stop and restart again. I thought about maybe reading all of Paul's letters this time because they were written to churches that were messed up or struggling (some were doing ok). So maybe I'd find some common ground. I did that for a good while.

The Crazy Story I Asked For

After that I wanted to find a church. I enjoyed the meeting I had been going to but I felt I needed more fellowship. So I started going to an English speaking church (keep in mind I was in Egypt where everyone speaks Arabic) that was called Heliopolis Community Church. The first day I was there, there was a guy preaching whose name was Dustin. I loved his sermon! He was speaking about how to pray the right things. I went to him after the service and told him I loved what he shared because I needed to know what to say to Holy Spirit. We ended up having coffee and (don't ask me how) he ended up becoming my mentor. It was great to have someone I could share with openly and who prayed with and for me.

I hope you guys aren't bored yet! The story is coming to an end soon.

Dustin shared with me about Luke Chapter 10:

[1]"After this the Lord appointed seventy-two others and sent them two by two ahead of him to every town and place where he was about to go. [2]He told them, "The harvest is plentiful, but the workers are few. Ask the Lord of the harvest, therefore, to send out workers into his harvest field. [3]Go! I am sending you out like lambs among wolves. [4]Do not take a purse or bag or sandals; and do not greet anyone on the road.

The Recipe

[5]"When you enter a house, first say, 'Peace to this house.'

[6]If someone who promotes peace is there, your peace will rest on them; if not, it will return to you.

[7]Stay there, eating and drinking whatever they give you, for the worker deserves his wages. Do not move around from house to house.

[8]"When you enter a town and are welcomed, eat what is offered to you. [9]Heal the sick who are there and tell them, 'The kingdom of God has come near to you.' [10]But when you enter a town and are not welcomed, go into its streets and say, [11]'Even the dust of your town we wipe from our feet as a warning to you. Yet be sure of this: The kingdom of God has come near.' [12]I tell you, it will be more bearable on that day for Sodom than for that town."

It was a passion of his that soon became mine. I wanted to be one of the ones that went ahead and prepared the way for Jesus to come. I really wanted Christians to be true believers.

I became active at the church. I served with the youth and developed an amazing friendship with the youth pastor Weston and his wife Amber (who are my best friends till this day). During one of our conferences I got to know Kim, a guest worship leader from Dallas, Texas. God spoke to her and her team before arriving in Cairo that they would meet a young man who would be a 'man of peace'. After she had led an awesome night of worship where I

got filled with the Holy Spirit, I shared with her my passion for Luke 10. She said that her eyes had been opened to me being the 'man of peace' her team had been told of. After an amazing chat, Kim became my spiritual mom. (We are still in touch and I travel to Texas every year to visit her.)

Jump in time.

On my first visit to Kim in Texas, we were sitting on her couch in the living room and out of the blue she asked me, "Peter, what is God telling you?"

I asked, "What do you mean?"

Kim, "I mean - what is God telling you right now?" I was baffled, "Nothing?"

Kim, "No! He is saying something. Just be quiet and listen."

I conceded, "Hmm, ok…"

I was quiet for what felt like hours waiting to hear God speak.

Nothing was happening.

Pause.

Kim wanted to me try and hear God, but I wasn't sure what to expect!

Was I supposed to hear a sound? See a picture?

Should I have remembered a verse from my Bible readings that would speak to me?

Maybe I needed to remember a sermon I'd heard such that God could speak to me through it?

Although I was still in the process of understanding how to hear God, there were times where I heard Him. I'm not sure how it was happening or how to explain it, but I knew I had to figure out the HOW. Not just for me but to share with others.

How can I expect to introduce someone to Holy Spirit if I can't tell him or her how to hear Him?

Chapter Three

The Recipe

I asked God to help me learn how to hear Him. I knew that if I were able to hear God's voice my relationship with Him would change dramatically.

I WILL BE ABLE TO HEAR GOD.

Think about all the times when you had no idea what you were meant to do… He is there to answer and you can hear Him!

I was taking my quiet time one day, reading a part of the Word and trying to think deeply, waiting for something to jump off the pages when I came across a verse that changed my life! It wasn't because He spoke to me through it, but because that verse was THE RECIPE.

God told me how to hear Him. It was a

revelation that opened my eyes (spiritual eyes). I wasn't just able to understand it and apply it, but explain it so that others could experience hearing God. It allowed me to hear Him, respond with understanding and easily enter His presence.

So do you guys want to know what I'm talking about? I want to share with you what the Lord has shown me. It is very simple. It has to be simple because He wants us all to be able to have a healthy relationship with Him… One that goes both ways.

Let's read together and I'll break it down, bit by bit... 1st Corinthians 2 starting from verse 10:

"[10]these are the things God has revealed to us by his Spirit. The Spirit searches all things, even the deep things of God.

[11]For who knows a person's thoughts except their own spirit within them?"

What Paul is saying is that our spirit (little 's') knows us best. Our spirit knows how we feel, what we think and the past and the present... it's always there (obviously).

"In the same way no one knows the thoughts of God except the Spirit of God."

God created us and gave us a spirit by which

we live and function which is a reflection of His image. He too has a Spirit (big 'S') that knows Him, knows His past, present and future and understands what He feels and what He thinks. I know we struggle sometimes with trying to understand the trinity and may think that the persons of the trinity are mentioned according to their importance or position, but keep in mind that they are one and equal.

"[12]What we have received is not the spirit of the world, but the Spirit who is from God, so that we may understand what God has freely given us."

So! As believers we have received the Holy Spirit, which is God's Spirit. He is in God. Let's focus now. The Spirit that is in God and knows God is now in us as well. This creates a connection such that the Holy Spirit now understands God and us. We said no one knows man better than his spirit so as a result the Holy Spirit that is in God and in us allows God to know how we feel and what we think as well as allowing us to HEAR AND FEEL WHAT GOD THINKS AND FEELS!

BOOM! Mind blown.

I have access to His thoughts and feelings because I have His Spirit that knows Him best.

Am I the only one getting blown away by this? It's awesome, right! (haha)

"¹³This is what we speak, not in words taught us by human wisdom but in words taught by the Spirit, explaining spiritual realities with Spirit-taught words."

If the Holy Spirit receives thoughts and feelings from God and wants us to understand them the same way God is thinking and feeling them, what do you think is the best way for Him to deliver the message?

I believe the best way is to deliver them the same way He received them. He will give them to us as thoughts and feelings! So when we try to hear God, the Holy Spirit is not necessarily speaking in an audible voice as much as He is giving us His thoughts in the form of thoughts and His feelings in the form of feelings.

"¹⁴The person without the Spirit does not accept the things that come from the Spirit of God but considers them foolishness, and cannot understand them because they are discerned only through the Spirit. ¹⁵The person with the Spirit makes judgments about all things, but such a person is not subject to merely human judgments, ¹⁶for,

"Who has known the mind of the Lord so as to instruct him?"

But we have the mind of Christ."

Paul ends with a small condition. We need to be of the Spirit in order to be able to hear and receive from the Spirit. What that means is that we need the Holy Spirit to take full control. Without the Spirit transforming us into 'spiritual' people we can't have what is of the Spirit.

Let me explain…

Before Jesus went into the desert, the Holy Spirit came upon Him in the form of a dove but when He came out He was filled with the Spirit. If you don't understand the difference it may be hard or even impossible to connect with the Spirit. Let the Holy Spirit take over! If you are wondering how, I will share with you shortly. Just know, being filled with the Spirit means that Holy Spirit takes control and as a result He gives you His characteristics. The most basic one being, hearing God's voice or, to be more accurate, thinking His thoughts and feeling His feelings!

Isn't that awesome? We have access to God's thoughts through His Spirit. We were always designed to have His Spirit in us. He wants us to be in a TWO-way relationship with Him but we may not have tapped into it yet. For me it was amazing to discover that He wanted me to know his thoughts, to know His feelings, to be connected... Get this please! We share the same Spirit! (Holy Spirit)

Holy Spirit has a very important role. Sometimes we overlook Him, Yes Him! I think sometimes we forget He is a He. Without understanding His role and authority we miss a crucial element of our relationship with God. What Holy Spirit does is He allows us to connect with God as friends (or sons) and without Him we are servants or at least we act like it. Holy Spirit allows us to see what God is doing all around us, where He's moving and how He does what He does so we can join Him in his work!

Let me put it all together.

We are always accompanied by our spirit, which means it knows us best. This is the same with Holy Spirit - He knows God best. So when we receive Holy Spirit into our lives and give Him full control (become filled with the Spirit) we start seeing His gifts and character rub off on us. The first of these is being able to experience God's thoughts through Holy Spirit taking God's thoughts and delivering them to us. We receive His thoughts in the form of thoughts and that is why sometimes we are thrown off by the word hearing (which isn't wrong). We get to think God's thoughts and feel his heart.

Now guess what? It doesn't stop there. Stuff keeps rubbing off on us. It's a process. When we remain in this relationship we receive more and more. I encourage you to go read 1 Corinthians 12 - 14. It talks about the amazing fruits and gifts that come with this relationship. You have the privilege of being a part of all of this, and yes it's all possible!

Chapter Four

The Map

I know that y'all have some questions like; How does this work?

How do I know if my thoughts are from God and not me?

How do I get filled with the Spirit?

How do I know that Holy Spirit is in control?

These are all questions I asked myself while I was learning to hear God's voice and this chapter is called the map because it will help you apply the recipe and navigate your way into God's presence.

Remember, I used to be religious without truth. It was more like knowing Him but denying his power and I didn't want to live that way again so I needed answers to my questions. I believe that Holy

Spirit is a good teacher and it is ok to ask! But be open for your mind to be transformed. I wanted to know the truth and be real with God but I also made sure I wasn't stubborn and was open to learn and change the way I think. We aren't always right!

So let's take one step at a time.

Step One:

Invite Holy Spirit into your heart

If you've already given your life to Jesus then you've already received the Holy Spirit but what I am inviting you to do is a little different. It means inviting Holy Spirit to not just live in you but to take control, to be the leader and to be the one who guides your heart, mind and senses. I know I have mentioned it earlier but when Jesus got out of the water after John baptized Him the word says the Holy Spirit rested on Him in the form of a dove. However, when he came out of the desert, the word says He was filled. The key is in the wording. He was so full on the inside, Holy Spirit started to overflow to the outside and that's what we want!

Let's ask the Holy Spirit together. Pray this prayer with me:

Thand you God for Your love and the purposes

that You have for my life. I know that You always planned to have a close, personal and practical relationship with me. Holy Spirit, I invite you to come over me, fill me so that I may overflow with Your presence in my life. Holy Spirit take control now. Take control of my life and my heart. Have Your way with me, lead me and guide me. Open up my inner man to be sensitive to You so that I would decrease and You would increase. Take control of me, Amen.

I want you to know that Holy Spirit is waiting for you. He has been ready for quite some time. And yes, it just takes a prayer. You need to ask and He will provide. Remember when I was sharing about Dustin's sermon regarding praying the right prayers- this is always a right one!

Step Two:

State the truth about God

It is important for you to be aware of God's desires. He desires a relationship with you. It is easy for you to create your own image of God based on what you've seen from your parents or leaders who are not true representations of who He is. God wants to spend time with you, to hear your voice. He wants to share with you the plans He has for you because

He sees you as a friend and not a slave.

For me it was a small short prayer I kept praying:

Lord I know that You are interested in me and want to talk to me. Thank you for seeing me as a friend and not a slave. Thank you for seeing me as a son whom you love and long to spend time with. Transform my mind that I might truly believe that I am a son and actually live like one.

Amen.

Step Three:

Kick Satan Out

How do I know that I'm hearing God and it isn't Satan or just my imagination? Well, there are two things that helped me answer this question.

God wants to talk to you and has been waiting (step two) and His voice and presence is stronger than Satan's. He doesn't want to confuse you.

So what we need to do is simply ask Him to protect our minds from Satan's words of accusation so that we would be able to hear Him clearly. If you're worried you're imagining things, ask Him to sanctify your thoughts too. You'll begin to discern what's from you and what's from Him.

And again just lift up a prayer:

Lord, I want to speak to you and hear you share with me. So, in the name of Jesus, who gained victory at the cross, I ask that you would protect my mind, imagination and emotions to be only from you in the next few moments as You and I spend time together. I declare that Satan has no power over me as I sit with You Lord because this time is for You and I, Father and son. Not for the enemy to join. I believe in the power of the blood of Jesus to protect, Amen.

Step Four:

Share and then ask Him to speak

It's simple. Just start talking to God. Tell Him;

What's on your mind
What your day was like
What's concerning you
What keeps you up all night
What you're thankful for Your deepest secretsWhat brings you shame
What scares you the most
What is hurting you.

I remember one time I told Him that I felt I didn't really love Him. This time is for you to talk!

Talk and don't worry about being judged because you are meeting with the wisest, kindest, most loving, most merciful, awesome, sweetest person that you will ever meet or talk to. He knows it all. The Spirit (Holy Spirit) in you already told Him about it all. Don't worry He won't be surprised. He just wants you to open up and share with Him. Sharing is like opening the doors of the secret places of your heart, yes He already knows about them, but now His light can come in.

Step Five:

Shut up and Listen

Remember when I was sharing about Kim helping me listen and I paused the story? Well, press play.

I closed my eyes and asked Him to speak to me. I gave Him control because I wanted Him to speak. I was quiet and tried to clear my head. Suddenly, a spontaneous flow of thoughts rushed through my head! There was so much going on!

He started to speak and I was able to hear Him.

It was God speaking His thoughts into my head. The first thing that came to mind was my sin but suddenly I saw a picture of a conversation between

Him and I and He was speaking about why my sin didn't define me and that He wanted me free. It was simple but real. And I knew it was Him.

Think about a first date... It's just like that but a LOT better. The next time I sat with Him was that same night. I asked Him to compensate for the years I had missed without being able to hear Him and He just opened the gates of heaven. It was amazing! The more time I spent with Him, the more frequent He spoke. It felt like no time had been lost. Within weeks our conversations had become immensely detailed – it was glorious!

I lay flat on my bed that night and looked at the ceiling. I smiled and said out loud to myself, "He speaks and I can hear Him!"

Right away He gave me a picture. It was a little scary but gave me joy. It was a picture of Satan falling on his face in defeat. Satan had just lost a major battle! From that day on, every time Satan came against me I had a great advantage - I CAN HEAR GOD! What on earth can he do? God had already won and I was on the winning team!

Chapter Five

The Tools

My experience hearing God was amazing. It was more than a high for me and I never wanted it to stop. I wanted it to become a part of my identity. I knew that Satan just had a major defeat, which meant that he would try to come back and steal what I had been given. I needed to make sure that I was always standing in the same place with a two-way connection with God. "Holy Spirit don't stop talking to me because I can't get enough and Your love is better than wine."

Well, there are a few tools that I wasn't given right away but had to figure out. They work very well in keeping this victory over Satan and because of them I have held onto my promised land.

I want to tell you first where I got them before I

share what they are. I got them from Hannah, my wife and best friend. Hannah was born and raised in Australia but of an Egyptian background like myself. We met in Cairo while we were both visiting as I had moved to Canada after finishing my engineering degree. Hannah spent a year there after finishing medical school and I was there because my friends Weston and Amber were having their first baby in Cairo when the revolution was happening so I felt the need to be there to protect the crazy Americans!

Anyway, Hannah and I only met three or four times in Cairo but after I left we kept in touch and became really close friends. She was even giving me advice when I was trying to date a girl I met, Haha. That's what I call a true friend! I grew close to her and was able to see how she was always connected to Holy Spirit and could hear Him so clearly. We started to share with each other and I noticed "the tools" she was using and how effective they were in keeping the land the Lord had given us!

So here we go…

The Tools

Tool One:

Spirit vs. Flesh

I believe most of us are familiar with the idea that Paul was talking about in Romans - spirit vs flesh. There is a constant tension between the two. Now, based on the recipe, we need to make sure that our spirit is winning the battle. Let me remind you of the last ingredient.

"¹⁴The person without the Spirit does not accept the things that come from the Spirit of God but considers them foolishness, and cannot understand them because they are discerned only through the Spirit. ¹⁵The person with the Spirit makes judgments about all things, but such a person is not subject to merely human judgments"

So what is being said here is that when we are of the Spirit, when the dominant side is the Spirit, it becomes easier for us to receive from the Spirit. Hannah was always making sure she was a person of the Spirit, which made it easy to understand what God was saying. She was using the first tool... fasting.

Ya, I know it can be annoying. I feel the same, but guess what! Sometimes we do it wrong.

For me it was annoying because I had to starve

The Recipe

myself till 6pm everyday, or worse, stay away from meats and sweets! I was more concerned with the diet change which was never the point. I will make it short and sweet. You need to find what feeds the flesh - and it's not simply about nutrition! Go eat well and work out but fast from what makes your mind "unspiritual". Remember how He speaks through our thoughts? We need to keep the receiver clean. I filled my mind with TV shows and movies like nobody's business. So, when I closed my eyes and cleared my head, guess what came to mind? The stuff I'd been watching. Not only so, but it opened my mind up to sexual attack.

Look guys.

Long story short.

I still enjoy watching movies and playing games but it isn't about that. It's about that which dominates your time and hence dominates the fight between spirit and flesh.

Hannah was always able to see when she needed to help the Spirit. I would spend three days without games or shows and read a book or study one.

Notice.

I didn't just stop something; I replaced it with

something that fed the Spirit.

Tool Two:

Da' Word

Hey, come on. Don't give me that look! You know you need the word.

It was through reading God's word that I was able to know Him more. I promise you it is going to be different this time. You want to know why? Simply because this time you can hear Him! He will explain His word to you. Hannah always reads the Bible at anytime! (If that sentence didn't make sense, let me rephrase it - she reads whenever she can. Not based on a set time). She is always waiting to hear something new.

Honestly, Holy Spirit has opened my eyes to a lot of truth that I would never have seen had I not read His word.

A very important element is being familiar with the word of God. Let it be continually on your lips, let it fill your thoughts. When you hear Him speak, a lot of the time, knowing His word allows you to discern what He is saying - its deeper meaning, the direction in which He is leading you and where to meditate in the word in order to find out more! This way you are confirming what you are hearing. He doesn't change and what He says will never conflict with what He said in the past.

I know this might be a stretch for some of you but meditating on the word and praying the word are dimensions that will allow for the voice of the Lord to be like David describes - like the sound of many waters. It's easy to do with the Psalms. After reading through a Psalm, switch around the words and pray it back to God. Make declarations over your life. Highlight the words that depict your longings the most and meditate on them. Keep repeating them and ask Holy Spirit to show you more. You will find yourself hearing God preach about God in a whole new way!

Tool Three:

The Gang

Hannah and I have been leading a youth group at a local church close to where we live in Toronto. We wanted to help the youth grow together and one of the effective things we started was a home group called 'F cubed' which stands for 'Fun, Food and Fellowship'. It has become a place for the youth to open up and share about what they're going through and learn together how to work through hard times.

We've had the chance to discuss some great topics, confess, share, grow, learn and understand. It's a safe place for them to unravel their hidden sins, reveal them to the light and stand together against common sins. Everyone needs a group with whom they can share their journey, discover who God is and who they are. You need to surround yourself with people who won't say the right 'church answers' (to be honest that builds no one). They need to be open about their weaknesses and allow God to speak and transform them from glory to glory.

One thing I've experienced for myself is the power of having people praying for you, people who receive revelation from God about you and then share it with you and declare it as truth over your life. Wow!

It feels awesome and makes you feel God's love in a very tangible way.

Fun and food is a big part of it. We need to have life together! I am sure Jesus and the disciples had moments around the fire talking about of the time when Peter burnt dinner or when John kept asking Jesus to make him fly and Jesus told him he had to learn how to swim first. (I hope you are getting the point). Find a group! It doesn't have to be a huge number, but be close to them and have life together. I know we can get busy with life but remember to give the Spirit dominance.

Tool Four:

Seeing the Unseen

The fourth tool is simply being able to see where God is working and join in with Him, which means being open to experience the mix between the two realms; the spiritual and the physical. A lot of people are unaware of what is happening in the spirit which puts them at a disadvantage. God wants to open our eyes in order to see what He has in mind for us.

We are co-workers and friends and He is at work in our lives right now. Didn't He say that the harvest is plenty but the workers are few? Well, He is working and waiting for you to join. Being able to see what God is doing helps you align yourself with Him rather than aligning yourself with the suffering you see and trying to 'convince' God to do something about it. He will guide you through this process.

I'll share with you a short story that should explain what I'm trying to say. A few years ago, right before I moved to Canada, counting down the days to my flight, I was bored at home and decided to go out and watch a movie. So, going down the stairs I saw the security guard for our building sitting by the door.

I said, "Hey Reda, how are you?"

Reda replied, "Well, life is hard so I guess pray for me!" I told him I would and kept moving towards my car. But then I remembered this tool and thought maybe I need to ask him a few more questions.

I went back inside and asked him why he wasn't doing well. Reda opened up as if he had simply been waiting for someone to ask. He was going through a lot. I asked Reda if he would like me to pray for him and he said, "Yes, Please."

Reda and I went to the roof and I asked him to start praying and then I would pray for him.

But he said, "I am a bad person, Peter, I can't pray to God!"

Tell me that you don't think that God was at work! He wanted someone to help Reda and even though it only took me a second I was able to see where He was working and join Him. I explained to

Reda Jesus' love for him and, unlike my story in chapter one, Reda gave his life to Jesus and every time he saw me that week he let me know what he had been praying and how great he felt.

Don't you love it when God does that! His plan is for you to join Him and be able to partake in the work He is doing.

I pray that these tools would help you advance in your relationship with the Lord and be able to not only hear Him once but always and partner with Him in His work.

Chapter Six

A Heart that is Eternal

I hope by now that you can see the big picture.

I believe that God is eager to speak with you and maybe you've already started following the recipe and the map and HAVE heard Him!

God has a purpose for our lives. It isn't just to learn how to hear Him; actually hearing Him is not the endpoint. It is a basic need to communicate with Him. Maybe you've never heard Him speak but you've seen Him work in your life. So, how much more will you now be able to follow and witness His purposes for you?

When God created Adam He was after a relationship. He wanted someone to connect with who had the freedom to choose Him like He chose

The Recipe

them. He breathed and with that breath He gave Adam life and a part of Himself! You and I have a piece of Him in us. We were designed with a heart that is eternal. That seeks to be satisfied with eternity.

Solomon had figured it out, in Ecclesiastes 3:10-11

"I have seen the burden God has laid on the human race. [11]He has made everything beautiful in its time. He has also set eternity in the human heart; yet no one can fathom what God has done from beginning to end."

We can try to seek things to satisfy our heart, but it won't work. Our hearts have a hole that can only be filled with eternity and who else is eternal but Him?

So, we have a part of Him inside us and a heart that is only satisfied by eternity and no one is eternal besides Him. It doesn't matter what you believe in, you were made to be in a relationship with God. You are connected to Him and that relationship isn't replaceable. No one can fill that need in your heart for eternity.

Now you have two choices.

Choice One: Continue to live life as usual

thinking that God is boring and that you know how to have fun by running to people, relationships, drugs, sex, movies, money, career…etc. You're hoping that one of those things would fill that need, that gap. You are trying to find your purpose away from the source. You are hoping that one day you will reach a point where you will feel your life is worth something.

OR

Choice Two: Understand how you were designed. What was God's plan for you? What purpose did He place on your heart? You were made to be loved by Him. Everything else stems from that truth. Choose to listen to Him, get to know Him better and you will discover the details.

Please understand that you were made to be in a relationship with Him, to have life together with the body, to learn the truth about what your heart really desires and understand that temporary pleasures will never be enough.

Finally, if you want to see Him in your life, house, workplace, church, country… you need to know that (as in Luke 10) you need to go ahead and find a place of peace and other men of peace. Together, you will pave the way so that He might be seen and glorified in the areas I just listed.

My prayer is that you would understand the value of His voice, the importance of His work and the blessing of partnership with Him. That way you will be in sync with heaven and bring His kingdom, as in heaven, on earth. Amen.

Scan the QR code to go to our website where you will find

- Book reviews

- Great deals

- Our full library of books

www.ingramcontent.com/pod-product-compliance
Lightning Source LLC
Chambersburg PA
CBHW031216090426
42736CB00009B/937